The new officers were installed and the work for the coming year planned.

Mrs. Legg served very nice refreshments, assisted by Mrs. Washburn.

CAPTURE 50-GALLON STILL

Sheriff Walter Ford of Morton county, and the sheriffs of Baca county, Colo., Cimarron and Texas counties, Okla., all took part in a raid and capture of a big 50-gallon still on Fred Plymell's place in Baca county, last Thursday.

Two men in a car, thought to be from Elkhart shot several times at the Cimarron county sheriff and his deputy, the shot taking effect in the car. Having a higher powered car they outran the sheriff's car and got away.

Several men were picked up in connection with this raid and at Andy Hargis' place, where a raid was made later. As there was no real evidence against them, all were released but Hargis, who is out on bond.

Miss Laura Hockett went to Macksville, Sunday, to attend the marriage of her sister, Miss Hess Hockett and Mr. Harold Combs, Monday. Miss Hockett and Mrs. Maricle returned home Tuesday.

Selected titles by the author:

In English:
Apocalypse Rose, Dave Haselwood Books (1967)
Neon Poems, Atom Mind Publications (1970)
The Last of the Moccasins, City Lights Books (1971)
Over the Stage of Kansas, Telephone Books (1973).
The Trashing of America, Kulchur Foundation (1975)
Blue Orchid Numero Uno, Telephone Books (1977)
Forever Wider, 1954-1984, Scarecrow Press (1985)
Hand on the Doorknob, Water Row Books (2000)
Eat Not Thy Mind, Glasseye Books/Ecstatic Peace Library (2009)
Tent Shaker Vortex Voice, Bottle of Smoke Press (2012)
Benzedrine Highway, Kicks Books (2013)
Incognito Ergo Sum, Ragged Lion Press (2016)

In French:
Choix de Poemes, Wigwam Editions (2007)
Apocalypse Rose (w/ music by Bill Nace), Lenka Lente (2016)

In German:
Moccasins Ein Beat-Kaleidoskop, Europaverlag (1980)
Panik in Dodge City, Expanded Media Editions (1981)
Liebesgesänge, Verlag Peter Engstler (2000)
Mindeater, Verlag Peter Engstler (2009)
Animal Light, Verlag Peter Engstler (2012)
Planet Chernobyl, Verlag Peter Engstler (2015)
Apokalypsenrose, Verlag Peter Engstler (2016)
Cat Man Do, Verlag Peter Engstler (2016)

Cowboy of the Ancient Sea

Leoncta, Ka

CHARLES PLYMELL

Cowboy
of the
Ancient Sea

Bottle of Smoke Press
New York

At the time of this printing, the following titles by Charles Plymell are still available from the original publishers. Many of his other titles are available through used and rare book dealers.

Hand on the Doorknob: A Charles Plymell Reader
Water Row Books
waterrow@aol.com

Tent Shaker Vortex Voice
Bottle of Smoke Press
bospress.net

Benzedrine Highway
Kicks Books
kicksbooks.com/books.php

Incognito Ergo Sum
Ragged Lion Press
raggedlionpress.co.uk

Bloodshot Bill Sings Charles Plymell
Feeding Tube Records
feedingtuberecords.com
&
Bottle of Smoke Press
bospress.net

Bottle of Smoke Press
29 Sugar Hill Road
North Salem, NY 10560
www.bospress.net

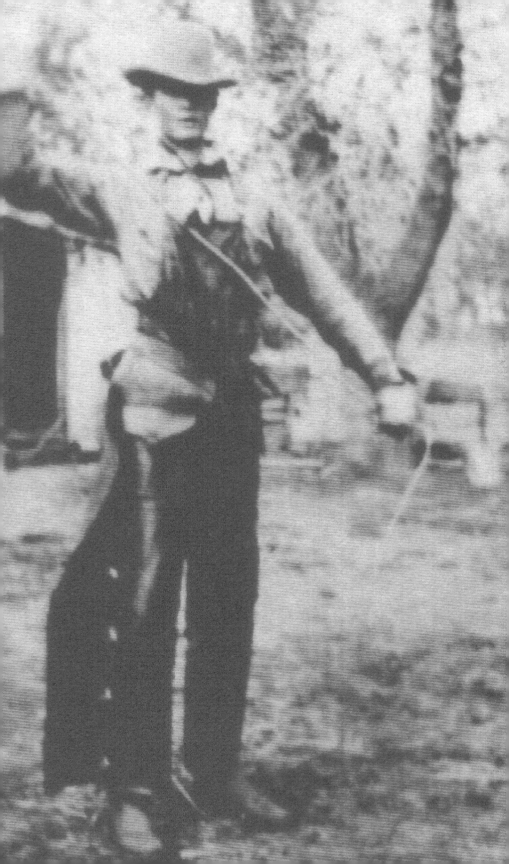

In Memory of My Father

To you who sung the riddles of that desolate Atlantis
while wind worn wagons swept a sunken trail into eternal dust.
To your sod, your grass, your easy hills of flint from glacial
slope to wanderlust. "Perfect cattle country . . . the best I've
seen since Uruguay." I'd oft heard you say, your dreams and maps
unfolded beneath those eyes that inventoried skies, could you
have known the winter owl's alarm where black beasts of Angus grazed?
I could not see as far, but went my way, you understood, and
watched the windmills tell their listless joy to silt and seam.
Life must be beautiful or all is lost . . . those bison of the clouds
were pushed from life . . . slaughtered for sport . . . now they are
the storm clouds watching us from eternity and far beyond.

And I did not know (when you showed me the lilies on the
limestone.) No . . . I did not notice you had grown old, your
hair had turned to silver . . . for I never thought you'd die.
I thought when this would end we'd all join hands together
like you told the babes at playtime long ago (that you hoped
we'd all meet in Heaven) in that dust bowl depression of Kansas.
It is hard to notice age in those who dream. As you knew,
dreams are like the youth, without them the world could not continue.
They are like the trees you always planted on sun-parched steppe,
enjoyed by those who pause and dream beneath the steel of time.
O fading America! Where is Thy promise! O catastrophic land!
This land you loved when newborn calf kicked up its legs . . .
you said everything wants to live . . . and expresses it.

The slap, slap, slap of tires on the grey concrete.
The tears on the way to the funeral. The biggest sky in Kansas.
"Wish I could find that old house where Grandmother lived,"
Dorothy said, trying not to think, or feel, or sob.
You had told me you "might kick off" one of these days,
but I could never see you anywhere but waiting for us
on the porch, arms folded always with finger prop't
against sunburned cheek, Stetson tipped back, calm grey
eyes anxious and kind through smoke of neglected cigarette.
We were coming for Christmas in a few short days with newborn babe.

Giant cranes along the ditch . . . steel helmet'd
construction workers laying concrete pipe beyond all
of the Family Store T.G. & Y. or the old folks home you cussed.
Under that vast space you saw the end products of wasted soul & hand.
You saw the time begin to change, you saw the Atom Bomb.
You knew the true nature of man, foresaw the greed and plastic goods.
Saw those old jaws of monster oil wells pumping never ending depletion
allowance of blood of man and earth. "The little man pays the taxes."
And you sensed the vacant stare in faces. You saw man change. You saw
him buy on time. But he had no time to talk now. No time. No time.
New car tires squeal on the road to nowhere to make a time payment.

Skull of memory, how will your lamp burn now?
How will the dust-like pages scorch that canopy of bone?
How will those eyes rest against the dark storm of tears now,
when ozone rests on sage, calming that stampede of time?
It was the day of mustangs, the day a train whistle screamed that
Rockies' grade, when double header highballed and howled past
diesel trucks, water towers of unknown towns; soliloquy of
settlements and cemeteries beyond truck stops and salvage yard.

It was said you paid the ambulance driver before you let him go.
You dug some bills from your old leather coin pouch to hand him.
Through your hard span of life, you settled up so quietly
no one ever thought of you carefully. Nor do they care for unknown sage
in an unknown town. The end of a man, an age. I neglected to hug or k

I was coming to see you from school, bringing my family.
Your father died with the fence unmended, the calves got out,
he didn't feel like riding; waited for you to come from school.
Everything changes but the meaning, and the tenderness passed on.
I stand here beside the peaceful grave, I stand here on earth
for the first time without you by me; I take this land upon my shoulders
The grain elevator over there is filled with wheat, the seed of
newborn day. The green Spring wheat. I am a father now. I know.

Your folks from Indiana came overland in covered wagons
crossed the Muddy at Hannibal Mo., Mark Twain was 36.

o Belle Plaine and on to "No Man's Land." You staked your
laim. I remember the joke about no birth certificate, and
ow the neighbors were healthy because they had government jobs.
Charley Dumbell shot himself with a Colt .45. You told the kids
ild stories, listened to Joan Baez, your favorite, with teenage kids.
ou were always young and built the fence for your daughter's horse.
ifting beams bigger than railroad ties . . . against the doctor's orders.

ost hole diggers left in the holes of prairie sod never used again.

FROM ANCIENT LAND (Vernal Equinox Dream)
Washington, D.C. 1984

They walked the sunrise, soul-burned travelers,
wearing hats tilted like Autumn's landscaped hills.
Rough-faced sailors, eyes laden like water rills
scanned the horizon till shore-lined stars unfurled.

New wind in the air for those wafting the seas,
new smell of earth dug away to align the leys*.
And they came forever wandering, as if set free
from cracks and rifts and vortices, as when some
great stone moves from its natural mortises; they
sailed the wind, a front of chaotic charges ignited,
careless in radiance of patterns of heaven unsighted.

(At 5:30 a.m. I awoke from a dream in Vernal Equinox
like a farmer called early for spring plowing, or a
driver with an early start knowing the aching miles
that stretch across the long heart of the prairie.)

*In the early days my father left his coffee pot
on the stove in his sod house, and he drove
cattle down to Galveston town, and he saw the
lights beckoning on the port side of the bow,
headed for Italy, brought back a color picture
of the Isle of Capri, and when he returned the
next year, the coffee pot was in the same place.
And the picture for years was the only decor in
the farmhouse room under dark cyclones rolling
with their terrible pitched-moan into stillness,
silent as trowels through the loess* and grasses
blowing dust through cracks of doors and windows,
sculpted the still waves day and night. The house
took in the wind of the wolves' howls, the song
of the coyote and the long train whistle dragging
the reptile's whispering scream of time, the pioneer's
pitch of desperation, first loud then soft, and
then distant into the stars where cowboys herded*

15

the dark clouds out of the sky, milkweed broadcast
seeds like stars while the bodies of wanderers
happily grew again from the earth's bed of gentle flag
and stay; the blossom'd buds in May blew like many
visitors who come when the new wind comes that
kept me half awake, half dreaming. . .so very many.

My father rode down through the equinox in a perfect
visioned dream as if he had never been away. I
wanted to show him the nation's capital, but he
was here on other business; he wanted to find his
merchant marine papers, why, I don't know, maybe
to show passage through eternity and beyond,
like a journey pulling toward yet another shore.

'Look at the beautiful masonry,' I said to him, 'look at
the Merchant Marine building with its exquisite work
of brick and tile, and bronze doors, and frontispieces.'
We went down to a little section of the city by the sea.
'Oh,' I said to him, 'this is just like Italy.' The marble
and the little streets and the glassworks and the women
who walked there, the women he joked with, and sailors,
and bricklayers, and the carpenters, and the threshers
from Kansas long ago, drifters passed in the street
recognized in memory, composite in chirality, patient
in formality; they, the lined-faced, the rough-hewn
people who walked the narrow streets by outdoor cafes.

He knew where to go, not up to the marbled entrance
but down a side street low, near a building, where,
in the dust of the sea bottom, beneath a small cupola
stood a woman by a counter of endless floating files.

'Draw me a picture of the last scene you remember
as a mariner,' she said. He drew a picture of himself
sitting on a bed, his sailor's hat cocked to one
side, a coffee cup on the table. He asked her jokingly,
'how do you want me, ma'am, hobbled and ironed?' She
helped him look. 'How far back?' He didn't know.
Down in the sea dust of a bottom drawer they found
his papers water stained brown. He pulled them out
and waved and yelled as if he had passage found
toward a wild fix of stars, shores on the Isle of Capri.

Notes: This poem was written when the poet lived in the Washington-Baltimore area. It was based on a dream he had at the time and date indicated.

* European Leys, archeological sites along astrological alignments perhaps tracing water holes and pagan rituals. Sometimes parts of gathered stones found in such places as Brittany. The author's forebears have been traced to a region near Ploërmel, France.

* loess, fine glacial sediment found in Kansas.

Allen Ginsberg had said IN MEMORY OF MY FATHER was one of the best elegies of the English language and Rod McKuen had done a recording of it. We lived in the D.C. area off and on while I was an adjunct professor in the many colleges. I had been offered two poetry courses at American University when Allen came to read there. I was interested in the poetry audience but had to turn down the courses because they conflicted with my scheduled English Composition courses I was teaching at "THE CUT" a maximum security prison between Baltimore and Washington. I told Allen I'd be at the reading and we could go for coffee afterwards in Georgetown. Over coffee and a generous hydrocodone from him, I showed him the addition FROM ANCIENT LANDS I had written from a dream on the Vernal Equinox at 5:30 a.m. It turned out that he also had written a poem about his mother from a dream at the exact time! He looked at the type-script, and though tired, edited it as he read. I remember him taking out the word, "perhaps" saying it sounded academic. His poem to his mother was published in the New York Times.

Port of SAN FRANCISCO

Jan. 4, 1921, 19____

I, _____ J. O. DAVIS _____, Collector of the District of SAN FRANCISCO, do hereby certify that the person described on page 2 hereof has produced such proof in the manner directed by law, and has hereby certify that the said person is a citizen of the United States of America.

Permission is hereby given the holder to depart from the port above mentioned.

This card must be surrendered to a Customs Inspector on each subsequent departure of the holder before he is permitted to depart.

In witness whereof I have hereunto set my hand and seal of office this ____4th____ day of ____Jan. 1921____, 19____

(SEAL)

_____
Collector of Customs

_____
Acting Deputy Collector

The person described on page 2 hereof has been examined by me, and having produced satisfactory evidence of American citizenship, he is hereby granted permission to land.

This card must be verified by an Immigrant Inspector on each subsequent arrival of the holder before he is permitted to leave his vessel.

_____
Immigrant Inspector

[SEAL]

Port of SAN FRANCISCO

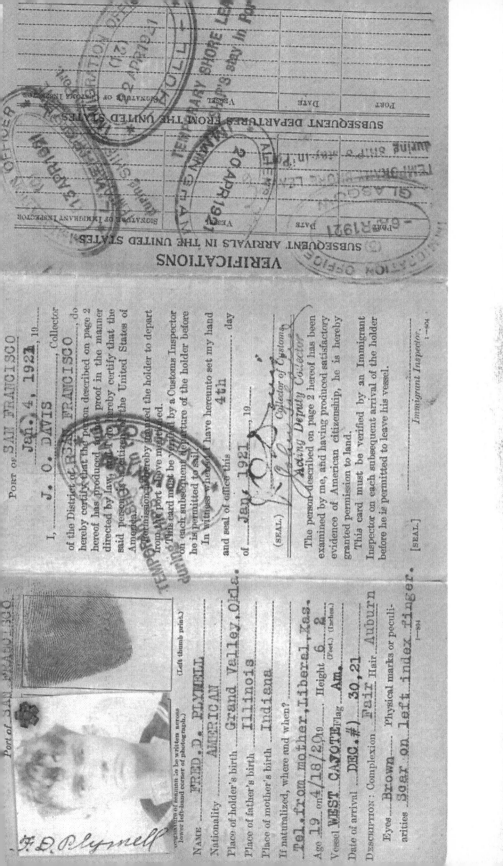

NAME ____ FRED. D. PLYMELL ____

Nationality ____ AMERICAN ____

Place of holder's birth ____ Grand Valley, Okla. ____

Place of father's birth ____ Illinois ____

Place of mother's birth ____ Indiana ____

If naturalized, where and when? ____ Tel. from mother, Liberal, Kas. ____

Age __19__ on __4/18/20__ Height __6__ __2__ (Feet.) (Inches.)

Vessel ____ WEST CAJOOT ____ Reg. __Am.__

Date of arrival ____ DEC. # 30,21 ____

DESCRIPTION: Complexion __Fair__ Hair __Auburn__

Eyes __Brown__ Physical marks or peculiarities ____ Scar on left index finger. ____

F. D. Plymell

(Left thumb print.)

About the Author

Charles Plymell was born on the high plains in Finney County, Kansas in 1935 in a converted chicken coop during one of the blackest dust storms of that period. His father was a cowboy born in the Oklahoma Territory, his mother of Plains Indian descent.

He is the author of over 50 books, broadsides, & records.

His poetry has been set to music by Bloodshot Bill, Bill Nace, Clubber Lang Gang, Cuz, Sam Dook, Mike Watt, Andrea Schroeder, & Grant Hart.

He lives in Cherry Valley, NY with his wife, Pamela Beach Plymell.

Photo credits:

pg. 2: Elkhart Tri-Sate News, Elkhart, KS, March 1, 1923

pg. 3: In front of Doby House

pg. 6: Holcomb, KS Fred with 5 kids and shadow of Audrey taking photo

pg. 9: trick roper at Plymell ranch in Palo Apache lands in Oklahoma

pg. 10: Father and son in Holcomb, KS

pg. 13: Threshers on the Plymell ranch

pg. 14-15: Fred at Mahoney's ranch, 1917

pg. 16: Fred at Plymell ranch Texas county, Oklahoma

pg. 20: Port of Galveston on West Cayote (Fred is far left)

pg. 21: Seaman documentation

pg. 22: Fred engineer on Union Pacific allowing Charley to pull whistle

pg. 23: Author photo by Bill Roberts

pg. 25: Robin Macy of Dixie Chicks in Belle Plaine, KS (Photo by Tom Av

pg. 26: Fred and Andy Gibson on homemade wagon, Plymell ranch

pg. 27: Fred "Let's go riding in the car car" -Woodie Guthrie

pg. 28-29: Fred's invented plow in Pierre, SD

pg. 30: Fred leaving his outlaw days behind

pg. 31: Fred later years in Belle Plaine, KS

1948-49 DAD WITH PLO[...]
IN PRATT, KANSAS. I HELPED

PHOTOS ON LAND
20 MILES N. OF PIERRE

LAND 4 SECTIONS (4 MILES SQ[...]

NVENTED AND ASSEMBERD
AND TRACTOR TO HIS

HIS '48 CHEVY IN BACKGROUND
WE HAD 8 48-49 REO TRUCKS C.P.

MILES N. OF PIERRE, S. D.

COLOPHON

This book was originally published by Bottle of Smoke Press in 2016 in an oversized, letterpress printed, edition.

This second edition of *Cowboy of the Ancient Sea* was designed and printed in North Salem, NY in March 2018. The text is set in 12 point Adobe Caslon Pro. Limited to an open edition of perfect bound copies, of which 25 copies are signed by the author and contain a laid-in photo of the author signed by the photographer.